John F. Kennedy

Michael Burgan

Chicago, Illinois

Edited by Adam Miller, Andrew Farrow, and
Adrian Vigliano
Designed by Philippa Jenkins
Original illustrations © Capstone Global
   Library Ltd.
Illustrated by HL Studios
Picture research by Tracy Cummins
Production by Victoria Fitzgerald
Originated by Capstone Global Library Ltd.
Printed and bound in China by CTPS

17 16 15 14 13
10 9 8 7 6 5 4 3 2 1

**Library of Congress Cataloging-in-
Publication Data**
Burgan, Michael.
   John F. Kennedy / Michael Burgan.
      p. cm.
   Includes bibliographical references and
index.
   ISBN 978-1-4329-8096-2 (hb)—ISBN 978-
1-4329-8097-9 (pb)
1. Kennedy, John F. (John Fitzgerald), 1917-
1963—Juvenile literature. 2. Presidents—
United States—Biography—Juvenile
literature. I. Title.

   E842.Z9B873 2014
   973.922092—dc23   2012037717
   [B]

Acknowledgments
The author and publishers are grateful to
the following for permission to reproduce
copyright material: Alamy p. 22 (© Everett
Collection Inc); AP Photo pp. 4 (Walt Sisco
/ Bettmann/Corbis), 32, 36 (Bill Hudson);
Corbis pp. 6 (© JP Laffont/Sygma), 14 (©
Bettmann), 21 (© Corbis), 26 (© Bettmann),
39 (© Bettmann), 47 (© Corbis); Getty
Images pp. 11 (Ralph Morse//Time Life
Pictures), 17 (Yale Joel/Time & Life Pictures),
20 (Gamma-Keystone), 25 (Ed Clark//
Time Life Pictures), 30 (Hulton Archive), 49
(Chris Smith/Contributor); John F. Kennedy
Presidential Library and Museum, Boston
pp. 12, 13, 27, 28, 35, 38, 40, 41, 43, 50;
Library of Congress Prints and Photographs
Division p. 45; NASA p. 34 (Kennedy Space
Center); National Archives and Records
Administration p. 18; Newscom pp. 8 (ZUMA
Press), 9 (ZUMA Press), 15 (akg-images),
31 (MIGUEL VINAS/AFP/Getty Images), 37
(akg-images), 46 (Tom Williams/Roll Call),
48 (HO KRT), 24 (akg-images); Shutterstock
p. 33 (Delmas Lehman).

Cover photograph reproduced with the
permission of John F. Kennedy Presidential
Library and Museum, Boston.

We would like to thank Andrew Warne for
his invaluable help in the preparation of this
book.

Every effort has been made to contact
copyright holders of any material
reproduced in this book. Any omissions will
be rectified in subsequent printings if notice
is given to the publisher.

Contents

Some words are printed in **bold**. You can find out what they mean by looking in the glossary.

A Death in Dallas

John F. Kennedy was just 46 years old when he was killed while driving through Dallas, Texas.

Cheering crowds lined the streets as a long, blue car rolled through Dallas, Texas. It was November 22, 1963, and people had come out to see the man inside the car, President John F. Kennedy. Next to JFK, as he was often called, was his beautiful wife, Jacqueline.

Kennedy had been elected president in November of 1960. He faced many serious problems when he entered office the following January. In world affairs, the United States and its **allies** were fighting the Cold War to stop the **Soviet Union** from spreading **communism**. (See page 19) Within the United States, Americans faced a weakening **economy**.

Kennedy had run for president promising to give Americans new opportunities with what he called a "New Frontier." This New Frontier would let people use their talents and meet new challenges, just as settling the **frontier** had let people do long ago. He told voters, "I believe the times demand new invention, innovation, imagination, decision." With him as president, Kennedy said, the United States could achieve "national greatness." Many Americans believed that Kennedy would fulfill those promises, and he had become very popular.

PRESIDENTIAL ASSASSINATION

Driving through Dallas, the president smiled and sometimes waved to the crowd. Suddenly, several shots rang out. The crowd watched with horror as Kennedy slumped over in the car. Two bullets had struck Kennedy, killing him instantly. Soon the whole world knew about the **assassination** of the popular young president.

John F. Kennedy's death shocked and saddened millions of people. After his assassination, people wondered what might have happened if Kennedy had not been killed. Would he have won the next presidential election? Would he have improved relations with the Soviet Union? Would African Americans have won the same legal rights they gained under the next president, Lyndon B. Johnson? Would the situation in Vietnam have been handled the same way? No one knows the answer to these questions. But even decades after his death, Kennedy remains one of the most popular U.S. presidents ever.

The Early Years

Jack Kennedy

Jack was the second child and second son born to Joseph and Rose Kennedy.

During the 1840s, more than 700,000 Irish left their homeland and sailed for America. Many were driven to go because of **famine** in Ireland. During that time, an Irish immigrant named Patrick Kennedy reached Boston, Massachusetts. He probably never imagined that one of his great-grandsons would become president of the United States.

FIRST WEALTH

That great-grandson, John Fitzgerald Kennedy, was born on May 29, 1917, in Brookline, a town just outside Boston. To his family and friends, he would be known as Jack. By then, the Kennedy family had become fairly wealthy. Jack's grandfather, P.J. Kennedy, saved his money and started his own business. His wife came from a successful Irish-American family.

Their son Joseph was John Kennedy's father. He did well in business too, first as a banker, then by making movies and other business activities. He married Rose Fitzgerald, the daughter of another wealthy Irish family. The Kennedys were not the richest people in Boston, but they were wealthier than most Irish Americans of the day.

A POLITICAL FAMILY

The Kennedys and Fitzgeralds were also interested in politics. Patrick Kennedy served for a time in the Massachusetts General Court, which makes the state's laws. Rose Kennedy's father, John Fitzgerald, was mayor of Boston and a member of the U.S. **Congress**.

John F. Fitzgerald
(1863-1950)

John F. Kennedy may have gotten some of his skill in politics from his grandfather, John F. Fitzgerald. As a boy, Jack went out with Fitzgerald when he ran for governor of Massachusetts in 1922. The Kennedy children also learned about American history from their grandfather. Fitzgerald was known as "Honey Fitz" because of his sweet, smooth way of talking to voters. JFK had the same skill to talk easily with people he met.

RICHES DURING TOUGH TIMES

By the 1920s the Kennedys were wealthy enough to own several homes. Wherever they stayed, Jack and his eight brothers and sisters played sports, learned to sail boats, and enjoyed their family's money. Most Americans, though, lived much differently, especially after 1929.

That year marked the start of the Great Depression in the United States. This huge economic collapse soon spread around the world, causing millions of people to lose their jobs and life savings. In some countries, such as the United States and the United Kingdom, governments set up programs, such as welfare, to help people who struggled to survive.

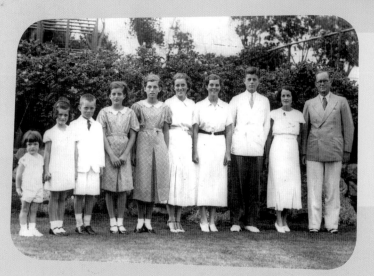

The Kennedy family visited London in 1937, shortly before Joseph took office as ambassador to Great Britain, in 1938.

TROUBLES IN EUROPE

In December 1937, President Franklin D. Roosevelt named Jack's father the new **ambassador** to Great Britain. The next year, Mr. Kennedy arranged for Joe Jr. and Jack to visit him. Jack also spent time in France, and he returned to Europe in 1939 to do research for school.

Joseph Kennedy hoped that his oldest son, Joe Jr. (right) would someday enter politics.

Having an interest in current events, Jack closely followed political activities in Europe. In Germany, a **dictator** named Adolf Hitler ruled. Italy's leader, Benito Mussolini, was also a dictator. Both men had built up their militaries, and Hitler had spread German control over parts of Europe where German-speaking people lived. Jack wrote letters to a friend, describing what he saw and heard. Much of it dealt with the chance that war would come to Europe.

Here is part of John F. Kennedy's family tree.

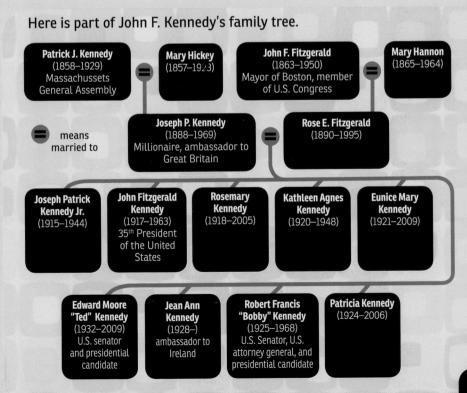

Patrick J. Kennedy
(1858–1929)
Massachussets General Assembly

Mary Hickey
(1857–1923)

John F. Fitzgerald
(1863–1950)
Mayor of Boston, member of U.S. Congress

Mary Hannon
(1865–1964)

means married to

Joseph P. Kennedy
(1888–1969)
Millionaire, ambassador to Great Britain

Rose E. Fitzgerald
(1890–1995)

Joseph Patrick Kennedy Jr.
(1915–1944)

John Fitzgerald Kennedy
(1917–1963)
35th President of the United States

Rosemary Kennedy
(1918–2005)

Kathleen Agnes Kennedy
(1920–1948)

Eunice Mary Kennedy
(1921–2009)

Edward Moore "Ted" Kennedy
(1932–2009)
U.S. senator and presidential candidate

Jean Ann Kennedy
(1928–)
ambassador to Ireland

Robert Francis "Bobby" Kennedy
(1925–1968)
U.S. Senator, U.S. attorney general, and presidential candidate

Patricia Kennedy
(1924–2006)

The War Years

Although Jack thought Germany would not start a war, Adolf Hitler had already made plans to invade Poland. In September 1939, German forces stormed that country so Hitler could seize land there. Great Britain and France had promised to help Poland if Germany invaded. Jack was in London when British **prime minister** Neville Chamberlain declared war on Germany. World War II was under way.

Joseph Kennedy was an **isolationist**—an American who opposed the United States' entering a second European war. U.S. troops had fought there during World War I (1914-1918). Some isolationists simply didn't want Americans to die in a war that didn't directly involve their country. Others thought banks and other private companies made money off of World War I. They didn't want that to happen again. The ambassador also didn't want to see his sons go off to war.

WRITING ABOUT THE WAR

As the fighting began in Europe, Jack returned to Harvard to finish his last year of school. For several months he worked on a 150-page report that suggested the British hadn't done enough to stop Hitler from starting the new war.

His father then hired several people to help Jack turn the paper into a book. Called *Why England Slept*, it was published in the summer of 1940. Major U.S. newspapers gave the book good reviews, as did some British papers. Some politicians and writers in the UK also praised Kennedy's work. Yet others thought the book would never have been published without his father's fame and money.

Members of an isolationist group called America First did not want the United States to go to war in Europe, and they held large rallies to present their views.

WAR COMES TO AMERICA

After the success of his book, Jack considered what to do next. He took a few classes at a university in California, then spent time in a Boston hospital for another illness. He felt better by the spring of 1941, and he traveled to South America.

Throughout this time, the war continued to rage in Europe, and U.S. relations with Japan were worsening. The Japanese, like the Germans, were seeking to conquer neighboring lands. Many Americans thought the country could not avoid war, and Joe Jr. and Jack **enlisted** in the Naval Reserve. Jack's health originally kept him out of military service. His father, though, knew a Navy captain who was willing to help Jack get in.

GOING TO SEA

Jack's first naval job had him working at a desk in Washington, D.C. He was in the U.S. capital on December 7, 1941, when the Japanese launched a surprise attack on the U.S. naval base at Pearl Harbor, Hawaii. The next day, President Roosevelt declared war on Japan. Jack requested to serve as the commander of a patrol torpedo (PT) boat.

In the Navy, Kennedy earned the rank of lieutenant junior grade.

THE PT BOATS OF WORLD WAR II

In the early part of World War II, PT boats made news for their speedy attacks on Japanese forces. The small boats were fast, but they also had many problems. They carried lots of fuel, which could easily explode if hit by just one enemy bullet. The equipment on board often broke down. And the torpedoes they fired were slow. The boats had to creep close to Japanese ships at night to hit their targets. But the men who volunteered to command PT boats wanted to show their courage. They also wanted to be independent. PT boats gave young officers a chance to be in charge of their own ship and make important decisions on their own. And Jack was probably already thinking about entering politics some day. Having commanded a PT boat in battle would look good to voters.

Kennedy and his crew pose on *PT 109*. The boat's bouncing on rough seas hurt Kennedy's back, which he had injured several years before.

DISASTER AT SEA

By March of 1943, Jack was in the South Pacific, where the Japanese and Americans were battling each other. On the night of August 1, Jack's boat took part in an attack on larger Japanese warships. In the darkness, one enemy ship slammed into *PT 109*. Later, Jack said he couldn't explain the crash: "It happened so quickly." Other naval officers questioned how alert Kennedy and his crew had been that night.

Two men died in the crash, and Jack worked hard to make sure he and the others survived. Through the night, the sailors clung to the floating wreckage of the boat. The next day, the men reached a small **atoll** almost four miles away. Jack towed a wounded sailor behind him as he swam.

Jack set out from the atoll to try to signal any PT boats that might be in the region, but that mission failed. Several days later, while exploring a nearby island, Kennedy and another sailor found two men who lived in the region. They gave the sailors food and water. Soon, Kennedy and his crew were rescued.

The U.S. Navy awarded Kennedy a medal for his actions after the sinking of *PT 109*. Here is part of the medal citation:

"His courage, endurance and excellent leadership contributed to the saving of several lives and was in keeping with the highest traditions of the United States Naval Service."

Kennedy receives the Navy and Marine Corps Medal while staying at a Navy hospital in Massachusetts.

BACK HOME

Jack stayed on duty through most of the year, but then stomach problems and a bad back forced him to return to the United States. He remained in the Navy until March, 1945. By then, his heroics the previous year had been described in several newspapers.

Before that, though, tragedy struck the Kennedy family, and it changed Jack's life forever. His brother Joe Jr. was killed in Europe. With Joe Jr.'s death, his father told Jack that he would take Joe's place in politics. Their father had planned Joe's political career for several years. By the beginning of 1946, Jack was back in Boston, preparing for his first political race.

While Jack Kennedy went to sea during World War II, his brother Joe took to the air. He became a pilot and flew bomber planes based in England. In August of 1944, Joe volunteered for a secret mission to help fly a radio-controlled bomber over German targets in France. The plane blew up before he could parachute to safety, and ended the life of a young man everyone thought would do great things.

Kennedy briefly worked as a reporter after leaving the Navy. He attended this conference in San Francisco, which officially created the **United Nations**.

Gaining National Attention

Although Joseph Kennedy wanted his son in politics, some of Jack Kennedy's friends thought he sought the same thing. Years later, Kennedy said he was drawn to politics because lawmakers "participate...in determining which direction the nation will go." He wanted to play an active role in shaping America's future.

John Kennedy describes the pressure his father put on him to succeed:

"My father wanted his eldest son in politics. 'Wanted' isn't the right word. He demanded it. You know my father."

THE CAMPAIGN BEGINS

Through the summer of 1945, Jack Kennedy once again traveled to Europe. When he returned, he gave speeches about what he had seen and heard. Those talks were good practice for the **campaign** he would start the next year. Kennedy knew that when he spoke in public he could sound dull. His speaking, though, would improve over the years, as he did more of it and gained more confidence. And even then, he had a sense of humor that helped him connect with voters.

In the 1946 election Kennedy was running to represent part of Boston in the U.S. **House of Representatives**. Kennedy belonged to the Democratic Party. Since Franklin Roosevelt's presidency, Democrats generally favored government programs that tried to help the poor and **middle class**. Democrats wanted to improve conditions for workers and increase health care. Kennedy said he would work to build housing for **veterans** and raise the minimum wage—the least amount of money a company could pay its workers.

During his first campaign, Kennedy said he was part of a "new **generation**" that included the millions of soldiers returning from the war.

The election process had two parts. First Kennedy had to win a **primary**. This election let Democrats decide who would represent their party in the fall election. That June, the Democrats in Kennedy's **district** chose him over nine other **candidates**.

SUCCESS AT THE POLLS

During the campaign, Joseph Kennedy spent several hundred thousand dollars to help his son get elected. But the younger Kennedy also worked hard to win votes. He rose early each morning to greet people going to work. Then he spent time knocking on doors so voters could meet him in person. The effort to win votes exhausted him, but it led to his primary victory.

In the next part of the campaign, Kennedy faced a Republican, Lester Bowen. The Republicans generally wanted to limit government spending, compared to the Democrats. Kennedy faced a much easier time against Bowen, since his district in Boston had many more Democrats than Republicans. In the November election, Kennedy won almost triple the votes Bowen did.

At the end of World War II, the United States developed the **atomic bomb** and used it on Japan. It was the most destructive weapon ever. During the Cold War, the Americans and Soviets tried to build more and better atomic weapons than the other side. This photo shows a huge cloud of dust and debris caused by a **nuclear** explosion, known as a mushroom cloud.

ON TO WASHINGTON

In January 1947, Kennedy went to Washington, D.C. Across the country, Democrats had not done as well as Kennedy had. The party lost control of the House and the **Senate** to the Republicans. Many voters blamed the Democratic president, Harry Truman, for the country's economic struggles after the war. Some voters also feared a new war could be brewing, this time with the Soviet Union.

As World War II ended, Soviet leader Joseph Stalin had helped communists come to power in most of Eastern Europe. Most Americans wanted to stop the spread of communism, and doing so might mean having to fight the Soviets. The growing tension between **democratic** nations, led by the United States, and the communist nations was soon called the Cold War.

Legend:
- Countries under communist control
- Communist but independent of Soviet Union
- The Iron Curtain

By the late 1940s, Europe was divided into communist and democratic countries. British politician Winston Churchill called the border separating the two sides an **iron curtain**.

During his 1946 campaign, Kennedy had spoken out strongly against communism and the Soviet Union. The vast majority of Americans opposed communism, but some Democrats did not fear its influence in America as much as Republicans did. Kennedy's tough anti-communist views sometimes put him in conflict with his own party's leaders.

LIFE IN THE HOUSE

Members of the House were concerned with communism and relations with the Soviets. But most focused on local issues that affected the people they represented. In Washington, Kennedy supported laws that limited how high rents could go and helped pay for school lunches for poor students. But at heart, Kennedy didn't like the government spending too much—especially if it spent more than it took in. Kennedy thought the government should have a **balanced budget**. With this stance, he sometimes conflicted with his own party, which believed that at times the government had to borrow money to pay for important programs.

The Marshall Plan

Under the Marshall Plan, U.S. goods and money helped Europeans rebuild their countries.

One government spending program that John Kennedy supported was the Marshall Plan. He and other Americans saw this as an economic weapon in the Cold War. After World War II, many countries were struggling to repair bombed-out buildings and rebuild their economies. Harry Truman and other U.S. leaders thought helping these countries would win their loyalty and keep communists from being elected. Stronger European nations could also buy more U.S. goods. Starting in 1948, the United States sent $13 billion to 16 European nations. These included not only Allied countries like the United Kingdom, but also Germany and Italy.

Kennedy also continued to battle back pain and illness. In 1947, doctors discovered he had Addison's disease. With Addison's, parts of the body called the adrenal glands don't produce enough of certain substances to keep a person healthy. People with Addison's must cope with weakness and stomach problems, among other complaints. Kennedy had to take medicine to treat the Addison's, but the drugs caused him to develop infections easily. He then had to take even more medicine. The drugs sometimes made his face look puffy, which can be seen in some photos of him.

THE NEXT POLITICAL STEP

Despite the ongoing illnesses, Kennedy was already thinking ahead. He was reelected to the House in 1948 and 1950. Then he began to campaign for one of the two Senate seats every U.S. state receives. Senators serve for six years, as opposed to two for a representative.

In 1952, Kennedy ran against the Republican senator from Massachusetts, Henry Cabot Lodge. The entire Kennedy family helped with the campaign. In the end, Jack Kennedy beat Lodge. Now he would continue to develop his skills so he could prepare for a future presidential race.

In 1952, Kennedy's bad back forced him to sometimes use crutches while campaigning for the Senate.

The Road to the White House

In some ways, Kennedy's victory in 1952 was surprising. He was young and not politically experienced, compared to Lodge. And Republicans had done well across the country, including winning the presidency. Dwight Eisenhower now sat in the White House. He had become a hero after commanding Allied forces during the invasion of France and Germany in 1944-1945. But Massachusetts voters liked Kennedy's charm, which made him seem like someone they could trust.

NATIONAL ISSUES

As a senator, Kennedy continued to speak out against communism. He worried about it spreading in parts of Asia, including Vietnam. He argued that the United States should strengthen its military and challenge the Soviet Union. Kennedy also refused to oppose one of the most **controversial** figures of the time—Senator Joseph McCarthy. The Republican had falsely accused hundreds of Americans of being communists. But many Massachusetts voters liked McCarthy, and Kennedy didn't want to anger them.

Kennedy won more attention from the **media** in 1956, when he was considered a vice presidential candidate for the Democrats. In the end, he was not chosen.

Joseph McCarthy
(1908-1957)

Senator Joseph McCarthy of Wisconsin first won national attention in 1950, when he said several hundred known communists were working in the U.S. government. For several years, McCarthy accused others of being communists, though he offered no proof. He also held hearings to try to find others he said were communists. This hunt for communists with little or no evidence came to be called McCarthyism. People who attacked McCarthy or defended people he accused risked coming under suspicion too. In the entertainment world, some people went to prison when they refused to give the names of communists they knew. Others lost their jobs if they seemed to support the rights of communists. McCarthy finally lost some support in 1954, when he questioned the political views of some members of the Army. The Senate accused him of misusing his power as a senator and it stopped him from holding more hearings. But some people's lives were already ruined after being falsely linked to communism.

To gain more national attention, Kennedy wrote articles that appeared in magazines. He also wrote a book that discussed past U.S. senators who had shown great political courage, such as John Quincy Adams and Sam Houston. Several others helped him write the book. Published in 1956, *Profiles in Courage* sold well. The next year the book won an important U.S. writing award, the Pulitzer Prize. The award boosted Kennedy's fame.

"...in the days ahead, only the very courageous will be able to take the hard and unpopular decisions necessary for our survival in the struggle with a powerful enemy..."

Excerpt from *Profiles in Courage*

RUNNING FOR PRESIDENT

Over the next few years, Kennedy wrote more articles and appeared on TV shows. More Americans were learning about the bright, charming senator from Massachusetts. At times he appeared with his wife, Jackie, whom he had married in 1953.

Young and attractive, Jacqueline Bouvier Kennedy helped JFK win support during the 1960 campaign.

As 1960 began, Kennedy formally entered the race to win the Democratic **nomination** for president. He called himself a moderate, someone who did not take extreme **liberal** or **conservative** stands on most issues. He traveled tens of thousands of miles and met voters at all sorts of places, from schools and theaters to restaurants and hotels. He smiled and shook countless hands, trying to convince Americans he should be the next president.

He also had to deny claims from another candidate that he had Addison's disease. Kennedy assured voters that he was in excellent health—even though the claim wasn't true. Kennedy didn't want voters to think he wasn't healthy enough to be president.

THE NEW FRONTIER

Finally, in July of 1960, the Democrats chose Kennedy as their presidential candidate. They picked Texas senator Lyndon B. Johnson to run for vice president. Once he won the nomination, Kennedy talked about the New Frontier (see page 5) and what he hoped to do as president. He was part of a new generation of younger leaders who had become adults during World War II. His generation had new ideas, unlike the older generation of President Eisenhower. The world was changing, Kennedy said, and America had to respond to those changes.

Millions of Americans watched Kennedy give his "New Frontier" speech on TV.

"The old era is ending. The old ways will not do...It is a time, in short, for a new generation of leadership—new men to cope with new problems and new opportunities....I tell you the New Frontier is here, whether we seek it or not....It would be easier to shrink back from that frontier, to look to the safe mediocrity of the past...and those who prefer that course should not cast their votes for me, regardless of party....I am asking each of you to be pioneers on that New Frontier."

Excerpt from the "New Frontier" speech, July 15, 1960

A CATHOLIC PRESIDENT?

Kennedy faced one major problem as he ran for president. He was Roman Catholic, and Americans had never chosen a Catholic president. In 1960, most people in the country were Protestant. Some Protestants feared a Catholic president would be more loyal to the head of the church, the pope, than to the United States. A few made even stronger anti-Catholic claims. In September, Kennedy spoke to a group of Protestant ministers. He assured them and the country, "I believe in an America where the separation of church and state is absolute."

THE DEBATES AND THE VOTE

At the end of September, Kennedy and Republican nominee Richard Nixon faced each other in the first of four televised debates. Nixon was President Eisenhower's vice president, and Kennedy wanted to suggest that Nixon was tied to policies that had weakened America.

As many as 120 million Americans watched at least one of the four Nixon-Kennedy debates. Nixon is seated on the right here.

Richard Nixon
(1913-1994)

Like Jack Kennedy, Richard Nixon had been elected to the House of Representatives in 1946. Both men spoke out forcefully against communism. And both, some political experts said, would do anything to win an election. After losing in 1960 and another political race in 1962, Nixon hinted he was leaving politics. But in 1968 he once again ran for president, this time winning. The Nixon presidency was marked by a political **scandal**. In 1973 he faced sharp questions about his role in a break-in at a Democratic Party office in Washington's Watergate building. Nixon lied about his role in the scandal, and in 1974 he resigned from office. He remains the only U.S. president to have left office because of legal concerns.

A NEW LEADER FOR THE 60's

KENNEDY FOR PRESIDENT

Kennedy's campaign tried to stress his youth and new attitude, compared to the much older Dwight Eisenhower.

In the first debate, Kennedy looked young, handsome, and in control. Nixon, partly because of makeup problems and health issues, seemed old and sickly. Voters who listened to the debate on radio thought Nixon won. But the millions more who watched it favored Kennedy. Nixon admitted that the debates helped Kennedy more than they did him. In the end, the election was close, with Kennedy winning just over 100,000 more votes. In January he would be heading to the White House.

Mr. President

Ice clung to the sidewalks of Washington, D.C, on January 20, 1961, and a cold wind blew. But the sun was shining and John F. Kennedy was in a good mood—he was going to be **inaugurated** president of the United States. The speech Kennedy delivered that day included one of the most famous lines ever spoken in U.S. politics: "Ask not what your country can do for you. Ask what you can do for your country." Kennedy believed Americans might have to do more than they had in the past to help make the country stronger.

Even political foes agreed that Kennedy gave an impressive inaugural speech, and it continues to win praise for its stirring language.

"Let every nation know, whether it wishes us well or ill, that we shall pay any price, bear any burden, meet any hardship, support any friend, oppose any foe, in order to assure the survival and the success of liberty."

From John F. Kennedy's inaugural speech

FIRST CONCERNS

All presidents assemble a **cabinet**, the heads of various government departments who serve as advisors. For the important job of **attorney general**, Kennedy chose his brother Robert, known as Bobby. In that job, Bobby served as the government's top lawyer and led a fight against **organized crime**. More importantly, he constantly gave his brother trusted advice. The rest of the cabinet included college professors and several business leaders. A president was not expected to only choose other politicians to help him. Two members of his cabinet were Republicans, a sign that Kennedy wanted some Republican views on important issues.

Robert F. Kennedy
(1925-1968)

Eight years younger than his brother, Bobby Kennedy managed his brother's 1960 presidential race. After JFK's assassination, Bobby stepped down as attorney general to run for the U.S. Senate. He won the race and began trying to aid the poor and those who struggled for equal rights. He also wanted to end the war in Vietnam, which had started under Dwight Eisenhower.

In 1968, while running for the Democratic nomination for president, Bobby Kennedy was assassinated, ending a promising political career.

LOOKING TO CUBA

As a senator and now as president, John F. Kennedy put a great deal of his focus on foreign affairs. The first world issue he faced was Cuba. The island sits 90 miles south of Florida, and for decades U.S. businesses played a large role in Cuba's economy. Then, in 1959, Fidel Castro led a revolution that threw out the government, which favored close ties to the United States. Soon Castro became friendly with the Soviet Union, which aided Cuba.

Fidel Castro remained in power in Cuba until 2008, when he turned the government over to his brother Raul.

Fidel Castro
(1926-)

Trained as a lawyer, Fidel Castro opposed the government that came to power in Cuba in 1953. He hoped to start a rebellion that year but was arrested and sent to prison. After his release in 1955, he spent time in Mexico and the United States, then returned to Cuba. He then began a rebellion that defeated the ruling government. After Castro seized power, he began to take control of U.S. companies in Cuba. This angered U.S. leaders, who stopped buying Cuban sugar, a main product on the island. Castro then began to seek closer ties to the Soviet Union and turn to communism. Over the decades, Castro tried to spread communism in Latin America and weaken U.S. power in the region. U.S.-Cuban relations remain tense today.

Fighters captured by Castro forces remained prisoners on Cuba until December 1962.

President Eisenhower did not want an unfriendly, pro-communist nation so close to the United States. In 1960 he ordered a secret mission to train Cubans who would return to their homeland and fight Castro's forces. Kennedy learned about this plan when he became president. His advisors debated whether to carry it out. Kennedy finally said yes, but he said the U.S. military would play only a limited role.

A FAILED INVASION

The attack on Cuba began on April 15, 1961. Cuban pilots in U.S. planes bombed Castro's air force, but did not do much damage. Kennedy canceled a second air attack when the public learned U.S. planes were used the first time. Two days later about 1,400 Cuban fighters began coming ashore at a spot called the Bay of Pigs. Castro's forces were waiting and quickly killed or captured most of the invaders. The Bay of Pigs attack was a complete failure.

MEETING THE "ENEMY"

In June of 1961, Kennedy traveled to Vienna, Austria, to meet with Nikita Khrushchev, the leader of the Soviet Union. The failed Bay of Pigs mission made Kennedy seem weak to the Soviet leader. Kennedy wanted to prove he was strong.

One tense issue between the two nations was the German city of Berlin. After World War II, the Allies had divided it into four sectors controlled by the U.S., Britain, France, and the Soviet Union. Berlin was in East Germany, which was under Soviet control. People seeking to flee communism there came to democratic West Berlin. Khrushchev warned that his country might cut off U.S. access to West Berlin. Kennedy cautioned Khrushchev not to stir up trouble in Berlin.

THE BERLIN WALL

In August 1961, East German soldiers began building a wall to separate East and West Berlin. The wall would stop East Germans from leaving their country. To Americans, the wall became a symbol of how communist governments denied people their freedom. In Washington, though, Kennedy and his advisors saw one positive sign in the building of the wall. If the communists were planning to fight over Berlin, they would not have taken the trouble of building the wall. The threat of going to war because of Berlin seemed to shrink.

After the Berlin Wall was built, U.S. and Soviet tanks briefly confronted each other, but no shots were fired.

THE FEAR OF NUCLEAR WAR

When John F. Kennedy and Nikita Khrushchev argued over Berlin, they knew a war would be terrible for both countries. Any direct conflict between the countries raised the fear of a nuclear war. Both countries now had weapons much more powerful than the first atomic bombs. Both had rockets that could send the weapons thousands of miles and planes that carried nuclear bombs were always in the air, ready to attack. A full-scale nuclear war could kill millions of people. Despite this danger, both nations continued to build nuclear weapons. In the United States, leaders counted on an idea called Mutually Assured Destruction (MAD) to prevent a war. The Soviet Union would not use its weapons first, because the United States would still have enough weapons to destroy the Soviet Union in return. Finally, during the 1990s, the United States and the countries that had formed the Soviet Union began destroying thousands of these weapons. The risk of an all-out nuclear war is much smaller today than it was during the 1960s.

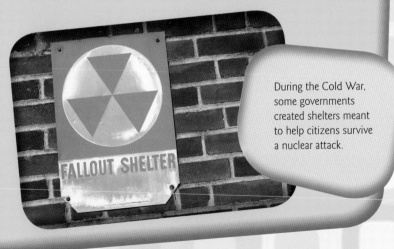

During the Cold War, some governments created shelters meant to help citizens survive a nuclear attack.

ISSUES AT HOME

Back in the United States, President Kennedy tried to strengthen the economy. To help it grow, he called for some increased government spending. That spending would help create jobs. But Kennedy didn't want spending to rise too much, since he didn't want to increase the **deficit** in the government's budget. Some people also wanted him to cut taxes. The president resisted at first, but in 1963 he did support a tax cut. Kennedy also introduced a law that raised the lowest wage workers could earn.

In general, Kennedy wanted good relations with business leaders—more so than some past Democratic leaders. Kennedy wanted to work together with business to help the economy grow.

RACE INTO SPACE

Some of the new government spending went into the U.S. space program. The Soviet Union had started the "space race" in 1957 when it launched a satellite. Soon after Kennedy took office, the Soviets put the first human into space. Some U.S. leaders feared the Soviets wanted to control space, so they wanted to match, or improve on, Soviet efforts. Though NASA got its start in 1958, Kennedy also saw a bigger space program as part of the New Frontier. The times called for new ideas and inventions. He wanted the United States to take the lead in space and impress the world.

As Kennedy had hoped, Americans landed on the moon on July 20, 1969.

> "I believe that this nation should commit itself to achieving the goal, before this decade is out, of landing a man on the moon and returning him safely to Earth."
>
> John F. Kennedy, calling for more spending on space research.

SPREADING PEACE

The space race became one part of the Cold War. So was a new program Kennedy supported. It was meant to help developing nations and show that the United States was not just a military **superpower**. Before winning the election, he talked about a "peace **corps** of talented men and women" who volunteered for several years in foreign countries. They would use their skills to teach children such subjects as math and English or to help the sick. Their efforts would help promote peaceful cooperation between the United States and other nations. Kennedy created the Peace Corps in March 1961. The Peace Corps still exists today, with more than 9,000 Americans volunteering in 76 countries.

Kennedy meets some of the first Peace Corps volunteers who served in Africa.

THE FIGHT FOR CIVIL RIGHTS

One issue at home had troubled Americans for decades. Since the end of slavery in 1865, African Americans had fought for the same legal rights as whites. Laws in some states, particularly in the South, made it hard for African Americans to receive a good education or vote. In the 1950s, Martin Luther King Jr. emerged as the leader of the **civil rights** movement.

Martin Luther King Jr.
(1929-1968)

Martin Luther King Jr. became a powerful leader of the civil rights movement. King believed that African Americans had to protest for their rights, but never use violence to do it. In 1963, he gave one of the most famous speeches in U.S. history. In this "I Have a Dream" speech, King hoped for a day when "my four children…will not be judged by the color of their skin but by the content of their character." King was assassinated in 1968.

In Birmingham, Alabama, police used dogs to attack black people during civil rights protests.

SMALL STEPS

During the 1960 election, Kennedy had promised to do more to help African Americans. Yet once in office, he saw that many Americans and lawmakers did not want much change when it came to civil rights laws. At first he took only small steps to help blacks. One was to have government agencies try to hire more African Americans. He also asked companies to do the same thing. But King and other civil rights leaders often wanted Kennedy to do more.

RACIAL TROUBLES

White opponents of the civil rights movement sometimes turned violent. In 1961, both blacks and whites known as "Freedom Riders" traveled to the South to try to register blacks to vote. Some Riders were severely beaten. Bobby Kennedy arranged for government protection for them. In 1963, violence also broke out in Birmingham, Alabama. A local police officer ordered attacks against civil rights protesters. This time, President Kennedy stepped in, asking Birmingham's government and white leaders to end the protests and violence. The two sides also reached agreements that gave blacks more rights in the city. Kennedy began to support more civil rights laws, but racial tensions remained in the years to come.

Martin Luther King Jr. gave his "I Have a Dream" speech in front of about 250,000 people in Washington, D.C.

FAMILY LIFE IN THE WHITE HOUSE

As president, Kennedy made important decisions every day. But he was also a father and husband. His daughter Caroline was born in 1957 and his son John Jr. was born soon after the 1960 election. The children helped make the president seem more like a regular father and not a powerful world leader. Americans were curious about his children, and they were often written about in magazines.

A loving father, Kennedy could not always play with his children as often as he would have liked because of his busy schedule and bad back.

Americans loved Jackie Kennedy too. Her popularity rose after she appeared on a TV show that took viewers on a tour of the White House (pictured below). Mrs. Kennedy explained the history of the building and showed some of the changes she was making to the rooms.

Jackie Kennedy
(1929-1994)

Well educated, pretty, and charming, Jacqueline Bouvier Kennedy seemed the perfect match for John F. Kennedy. Her knowledge of art and sense of style appealed to many people. Fashion designers copied what she wore so all American women could dress like her. Being **First Lady** was not always easy for Mrs. Kennedy. She did not like politics and going to public events. After her husband's death, Jackie Kennedy remained in the public eye. She married a Greek millionaire, then worked in publishing.

AWAY FROM THE WHITE HOUSE

As president, Kennedy traveled often, though not always for work. He sometimes went to the Kennedy family homes in Florida and Massachusetts. He also spent some time in California. His sister Pat had married a British actor named Peter Lawford. Through him, Kennedy met famous entertainers, such as Frank Sinatra. The stars gave the president a sense of glamour—he was like a star himself. In return, the stars enjoyed being connected to a powerful leader.

During some of Kennedy's travels he spent time with other women. Jackie knew this and mostly accepted it. The public, though, never learned about these relationships until years after Kennedy was killed. He also kept secret just how bad his health was. Each day, the president took medicine for his Addison's disease and other problems. A daily swim was one way Kennedy dealt with his back pain. The time in the pool also helped him relax.

MORE INTERNATIONAL CHALLENGES

As 1962 began, one **poll** showed that almost 80 percent of Americans approved of the job Kennedy was doing. By then, Kennedy was paying more attention to the war in Vietnam. Future presidents would see their popularity fall because of it.

In 1954, Vietnam won its independence from France, though the country was divided in two. North Vietnam was ruled by communists, while South Vietnam was more democratic and supported by the United States. During the Eisenhower years, communist rebels in the South received help from North Vietnam and from China, which was also communist. As part of the Cold War, the Americans sent increasing aid to the South, to help defeat the communists. American leaders believed in what was called the **domino theory**. If South Vietnam became communist, its neighbors would fall to communism too, the way one falling domino knocks down the one next to it.

Kennedy had specially trained U.S. forces wear green **berets**. The soldiers were soon called the Green Berets and carried out dangerous missions in Vietnam.

AID TO VIETNAM

Kennedy accepted the domino theory. Most of his advisors wanted him to do more to aid South Vietnam, including sending military troops. In November 1961, Kennedy decided to send more military equipment to South Vietnam. He also doubled the number of U.S. military advisors there. In reality, many of these advisors took part in combat, even though an international agreement was supposed to prevent this. Over the next two years, thousands more U.S. advisors went to Vietnam. They became more actively involved in the fighting, but Kennedy never admitted this. He did not want Americans to know that U.S. troops were fighting in Vietnam. News reports, though, showed that Americans were dying because of this distant war.

THE KILLING OF A PRESIDENT

John F. Kennedy often had difficult relations with President Ngo Dinh Diem of South Vietnam. Diem wanted U.S. aid, but he didn't want to follow U.S. orders. Those included giving the Vietnamese more political rights. By 1963, U.S. officials believed Diem couldn't be an effective president as the South Vietnamese and Americans battled the communists. Kennedy supported a group of South Vietnamese generals who were planning a **coup**. Diem tried to flee but realized he couldn't escape and gave up. Some of the generals then killed him. Kennedy had not expected this and the news of Diem's death shocked him. Kennedy also wondered if the new government would be any better at bringing true democracy to South Vietnam. In the end, it was not.

Bobby Kennedy worried about the effects of supporting the military coup against South Vietnam's Ngo Dinh Diem.

THE CUBAN MISSILE CRISIS

Toward the end of 1962, Kennedy once again faced a crisis in Cuba—and the world feared a nuclear war was at hand. That October, U.S. spy planes revealed that the Soviet Union was placing **missiles** in Cuba. These rocket-powered vehicles carried nuclear weapons. The Soviet Union saw the missiles as a way to protect Cuba from a possible U.S. attack. But Kennedy believed the Soviets might also use them to strike first against the United States.

The Soviet Union was bringing two kinds of missiles to Cuba. The most powerful could have reached most U.S. cities in minutes.

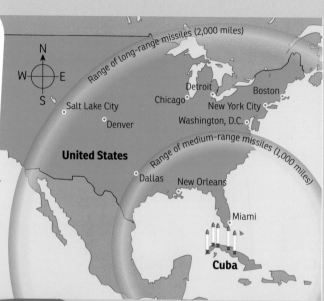

Range of long-range missiles (2,000 miles)

Detroit
Boston
Chicago
New York City
Salt Lake City
Washington, D.C.
Denver

United States

Range of medium-range missiles (1,000 miles)

Dallas
New Orleans

Miami

Cuba

"We will not...risk the costs of worldwide nuclear war in which even the fruits of victory would be ashes in our mouth—but neither will we shrink from that risk at any time it must be faced."

From Kennedy's address to the American public, October 22, 1962

Kennedy and his advisors debated what to do. All agreed the missiles could not stay in Cuba. But a direct attack on the island could spark the Soviets to attack West Berlin or use nuclear weapons elsewhere. Kennedy finally decided to begin a naval **quarantine**. U.S. ships would prevent Soviet vessels from reaching Cuba unless Nikita Khrushchev removed the missiles. If the Soviets fired any of the missiles, the United States would unleash its nuclear weapons on the Soviet Union.

TENSE DAYS

After Kennedy announced the quarantine, the whole world waited with fear as Soviet ships approached Cuba. Everyone knew that the world faced destruction never seen before and the death of millions of people—if the Soviets confronted the U.S. ships. Instead, most of the Soviet vessels turned away. The Soviets were not ready to risk a war. But they also didn't say they would remove the missiles. Then, on October 26, Kennedy received a letter from Khrushchev. The Soviet leader didn't want to fight, which Kennedy saw as a good sign. But when a Soviet anti-aircraft missile shot down a U.S. spy plane over Cuba, the fear of war rose again. Kennedy still wanted to end the crisis peacefully—as long as the Soviets removed the missiles. He proposed that if the Soviets removed them, the United States would publicly promise not to invade Cuba. In a second, secret offer, Kennedy would later remove U.S. nuclear weapons based in Turkey and aimed at the Soviet Union. Khrushchev accepted the deal. Kennedy showed his skills in **diplomacy**. He took strong action to achieve his main goal—getting the Soviet missiles out of Cuba. But he was also willing to give the Soviets something they wanted in return.

Realizing how close their countries had come to war, Kennedy and Khrushchev tried to improve their relations. In 1963, they signed an agreement that limited some testing of nuclear weapons. They also set up a "hotline" between Washington and the Soviet capital of Moscow. The two leaders would be able to communicate quickly in any future crisis.

During the Cuban Missile Crisis, Kennedy taped his meetings with advisors. These tapes give historians important information about the crisis.

Dallas and After

As 1963 went on, President Kennedy faced political troubles in Congress as he tried to pass a new civil rights law. Southern Democrats fought his efforts. Kennedy was still wrestling with that issue when he traveled to Dallas on November 21. Before he and Mrs. Kennedy left, he told an aide that his back was feeling good, and he might even ride a horse at Vice President Lyndon Johnson's ranch. Still, he wore a back brace that helped to ease his pain. And he never got a chance to take that ride.

THE ASSASSINATION

Along the route the Kennedys took through Dallas, Lee Harvey Oswald waited inside a book depository, a building where books were stored. Oswald worked there, and the building was on the parade route. That gave him a chance to commit one of the greatest crimes in U.S. history. Using a rifle, Oswald fired three shots, killing John F. Kennedy. The president's back brace actually helped cause his death. After he was hit in the neck by one bullet, the brace kept Kennedy's head up. That made it an easier target for Oswald's next, deadly shot.

Oswald was soon caught by police, but he never went to court. A few days later, a Dallas business owner named Jack Ruby shot and killed Oswald. The president's killer never had a complete chance to explain why he did what he did.

Meanwhile, just 99 minutes after JFK was dead, Lyndon Johnson became the next U.S. president. And word spread quickly around the world about the assassination of John F. Kennedy. In the United States, Earl Warren, the chief justice of the **Supreme Court**, wrote to Jackie that Americans had a duty to complete "the unfinished work of your beloved husband."

Jackie Kennedy still wore the dress with her husband's blood on it as she watched Lyndon Johnson become the next president.

WHAT REALLY HAPPENED?

Soon after the assassination, rumors began to spread. Some people claimed Oswald had not acted alone. Some said he wasn't the killer at all. Chief Justice Warren led a **commission** that studied the Kennedy killing. This Warren Commission went through records and interviewed hundreds of people. The commission also studied an important piece of evidence: a film of the shooting made by a Dallas resident named Abraham Zapruder.

The color film clip is just 26 seconds long—just long enough to show Kennedy being struck by the bullets. Americans first saw some images from this film in *Life*, a well-known magazine. The whole clip was not shown publicly for many years. But some people who did see it said the way Kennedy's head moved could mean he had been shot by two people in two different locations. The second shooter could have been on a grassy area, called a knoll, to the right of Kennedy's car.

Abraham Zapruder had first left this movie camera at home, then returned to get it so he could record JFK's trip through Dallas.

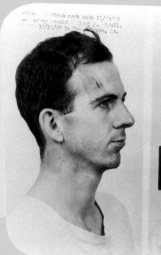

Lee Harvey Oswald had been in the military and was highly skilled with using rifles.

QUESTIONS REMAIN

The Warren Commission issued its report in September of 1964. It said Oswald supported communism, and he acted alone in killing Kennedy. Yet since then, many people have refused to accept this finding. Believers in a **conspiracy** to kill Kennedy point out that many people didn't like him. These included crime figures who hated Kennedy's efforts to end their activities. Also, Cuban leader Fidel Castro opposed Kennedy. One theory claimed Castro knew Oswald planned to kill JFK, but there was little evidence to support this idea. Or perhaps Cubans who hated Castro killed Kennedy because he had not done enough to end communism there. While many people might have opposed Kennedy's policies, it's not clear what they would gain from killing him.

"The Commission has found no evidence that either Lee Harvey Oswald or Jack Ruby was part of any conspiracy, domestic or foreign, to assassinate President Kennedy."

From the Warren Commission Report

A LASTING IMPACT

After John F. Kennedy's sudden death, many people saw him as a hero. In some ways, Jackie Kennedy helped create this image. She compared Kennedy's presidency to Camelot and King Arthur. Myths of this English king and his brave knights have been told for hundreds of years. Kennedy himself had read those stories as a boy.

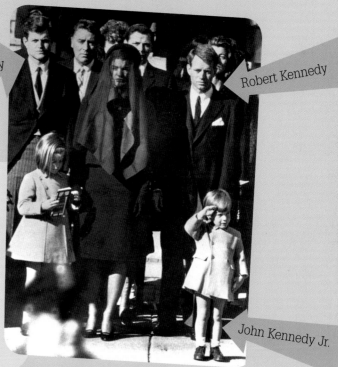

Edward Kennedy

Robert Kennedy

John Kennedy Jr.

After the death of his famous father, John Kennedy Jr. remained a public figure for the rest of his life. He died in a plane crash in 1999.

Historians carefully study all U.S. presidents. Kennedy has been praised for how he avoided war with the Soviet Union during the Cuban Missile Crisis. He created programs that offered positive change. The space program and the Peace Corps are two examples. Kennedy also used radio and TV like no president before him. Part of that, though, was his desire to control how voters saw him, so he could be seen in the best light.

Critics note that throughout his career, Kennedy relied on help from his wealthy father. Few candidates had the same support. And Kennedy did not always tell Americans the truth about his actions. The role of U.S. troops in Vietnam was one example of this.

Although he served for less than three years, Kennedy's presidency seemed to set a tone for the entire 1960s. He saw great changes in the world, and dangers. His assassination was just one example of the violence that seemed to spread as the decade went on. Today, he remains one of the most popular U.S. presidents ever. As one historian wrote, he "will always be remembered as a remarkable person, if not as a great president."

THE KENNEDY FAMILY

In 1968, the assassination of Bobby Kennedy stunned many Americans, just as JFK's death had in 1963. The Kennedy family, though, remained interested in politics. John's younger brother Edward, known as Ted, was already serving in the U.S. Senate. He would remain there until his death in 2009. Several of JFK's nieces and nephews also won elections. 2011 marked the first time in more than 60 years that no Kennedy held an elected position in Washington D.C. The Kennedys have served others outside of politics too. JFK's sister Eunice Kennedy Shriver helped found the Special Olympics, an international sporting organization and event for people with intellectual disabilities. The Special Olympics are distinct from the Paralympics, which are primarily for people with physical disabilities. Other Kennedys have been active supporting charities around the world.

Bobby Kennedy was killed in a California hotel while running for president.

What If?

Kennedy's health issues convinced him he would die young. Yet he was able to perform all his duties as president, thanks to many medicines. If Kennedy had not been shot, those drugs would have helped keep him alive. But no one knows for sure how taking so many drugs for so many years would have affected his body.

And no one knows what Kennedy would have done if he had won the 1964 election. Johnson easily won that election and the Democrats controlled Congress. Those victories helped Johnson pass laws that Kennedy had proposed on civil rights and education, among others. Kennedy probably could have also won the election, since the Republican candidate did not have wide support. JFK would have probably gotten those laws passed too. But he might not have proposed all of the laws that Johnson later passed.

The Vietnam War became the biggest issue for Americans during the 1960s. Kennedy did not want to fight a major war there. Some believe that he was planning to pull out all the U.S. troops. But Bobby Kennedy said in 1964 that his brother had not decided whether to pull out or send more troops. If Kennedy did not send more troops, as Johnson did, the United States most likely would not have faced the large protests against the war that developed later in the decade. And hundreds of thousands of people might not have died in the war that did take place.

Timeline

1917
May 29
John Fitzgerald Kennedy is born in Brookline, Massachusetts

1936
Kennedy enters Harvard University

1941
Kennedy enlists in the U.S. Naval Reserve

1943
August
As commander of *PT 109*, Kennedy helps save the lives of some of his crew after the Japanese sink his boat

1946
Kennedy wins election to the U.S. House of Representatives.

1947
Doctors discover that Kennedy has Addison's disease, which forces him to take medication for the rest of his life

1952
Kennedy wins election to the U.S. Senate

1953
Kennedy marries Jacqueline Bouvier

1956
Some Democrats suggest JFK should be the party's candidate for vice president

1957
Profiles in Courage, written in part by Kennedy, wins the Pulitzer Prize

1960
In a close race, Kennedy defeats Richard Nixon to win the presidency

1961
April
The failed Bay of Pigs invasion worsens relations between the United States and Cuba

1961
May
Kennedy announces his plan to put humans on the moon before 1970

1961
June
Meeting in Vienna, Kennedy and Soviet leader Nikita Khrushchev disagree on several important issues

1962
October
Kennedy convinces Khrushchev to remove missiles from Cuba, ending a crisis that could have come to war

1963
Spring
Violence breaks out in Birmingham, Alabama, as police attack civil rights protestors

1963
November 22
Kennedy is assassinated in Dallas, Texas

1964
September
The Warren Commission issues a report saying Lee Harvey Oswald acted alone in killing John F. Kennedy

Glossary

allies people or nations who work together for a common goal, particularly during a war; when capitalized as Allies it refers to the United States, the United Kingdom, and countries that fought on their side during World Wars I and II, including the Soviet Union during World War II.

ambassador person who represents the government of his or her country in a foreign nation

assassination killing of an important person, such as a political leader

atoll small island made up of the skeletons of living creatures called coral

atomic bomb weapon that uses the energy released by splitting tiny particles called atoms

attorney general top government lawyer in the United States

balanced budget economic plan that has a government spending only as much money as it takes in

beret soft, round, flat hat that fits snugly on the head

cabinet group of people who head different government departments and advise a leader

campaign process of running to win an election

candidate person running in an election

civil rights personal legal right to things such as voting and receiving fair treatment when applying for jobs and housing

commission group formed to study a certain subject over a short period of time

communism political system in which the government controls all large businesses, limits personal freedom, and prevents any challenges to its rule

Congress part of the U.S. government that makes laws; it contains the House of Representatives and the Senate

conservative in U.S. politics, someone who generally favors great individual freedom, especially in the economy

conspiracy secret plan carried out by a group of people to commit a crime

controversial tending to create both strong good and bad feelings

corps large group of people working for a shared goal

coup violent takeover of a government, often by the military

deficit amount of money a government spends that is more than what it takes in

democratic referring to a government that allows free elections of leaders

dictator ruler with total power over a country

diplomacy skill of making agreements between people or groups with opposing ideas

district area of a city or state with its own elected representative

domino theory Cold War belief that if one country switched to a communist government, its neighbors would too

economy total goods and services produced in a particular region, such as a city, state, or country

enlisted volunteered to serve in the military

famine severe shortage of food

First Lady wife of a U.S. president

frontier outer edges of a region, where few people live

generation group of people born at roughly the same time

House of Representatives larger of the two branches of Congress, with 435 members

inaugurated officially given a new title and powers

iron curtain phrase used during the Cold War to describe the border between democratic and communist nations in Europe

isolationist person who does not want his or her country to fight in foreign wars, unless attacked first

liberal in U.S. politics, a person who supports the use of government power to try to help the poor, promote equality, and limit business practices that harm society

media companies that provide information, such as radio and TV stations

middle class large number of people in a country that are not rich or poor

missiles weapons that are shot or thrown through the air; in modern times, weapons powered by rocket or jet engines

nomination selection of a person to represent a particular party during an election

nuclear relating to the core, or nucleus of atoms

organized crime groups of people that work together to carry out illegal activities

poll questions asked to see what people think about a particular subject

primary election held by a political party to choose its candidates

prime minister head of government in certain countries, such as the United Kingdom

quarantine effort to keep someone or something from entering or leaving a certain area

scandal activity that involves some kind of wrongdoing, and that becomes known to many people

Senate smaller of the two branches of Congress, with two senators from each of the 50 U.S. states

Soviet Union former country consisting of Russia, Ukraine, and 13 other current Eastern European and Central Asian nations

superpower nation with a massive military that it can easily use around the world

Supreme Court most powerful court in many nations, including the United States

United Nations group formed in 1945 to try to prevent wars around the world

veterans people who have served in the military

Find Out More

Books

Benoit, Peter. *The Space Race*. New York: Children's Press, 2012.

Corrigan, Jim. *The 1950s: A Decade in Photos*. Berkeley Heights, NJ: Enslow Publishers, 2010.

Cregan, Elizabeth R. *Independence and Equality*. World Black History. Chicago: Heinemann Library, 2010.

Isserman, Maurice. *Vietnam War*. Third ed. New York: Chelsea House, 2011.

Jones, Rob Lloyd. *See Inside the Second World War*. London: Usborne Publishing, 2011.

Langley, Andrew. *The Collapse of the Soviet Union: The End of an Empire*. Minneapolis: Compass Point Books, 2006.

Mara, Wil. *John F. Kennedy*. New York: Marshall Cavendish Benchmark, 2010.

Morgan, Kayla. *The Cold War*. Edina, MN: ABDO Publishing, 2011.

Sandler, Martin W. *Kennedy Through the Lens: How Photography and Television Revealed and Shaped an Extraordinary Leader*. New York: Walker, 2011.

Senker, Cath: *Days of Decision: Kennedy and the Cuban Missile Crisis*. Chicago: Heinemann Library, 2013.

Websites

American President: John F. Kennedy
www.millercenter.org/president/kennedy

The American Presidency Project: Audio and Video for John F. Kennedy
www.presidency.ucsb.edu/medialist.php?presid=35

BBC History: The Cold War
www.bbc.co.uk/history/worldwars/coldwar

John F. Kennedy Presidential Library
www.jfklibrary.org

Kennedy and the Cuban Missile Crisis
www.history.com/videos/kennedy-and-the-cuban-missile-crisis

The Kennedy Assassination
mcadams.posc.mu.edu/home.htm

Peace Corps
www.peacecorps.gov

DVDs

Cold War.
Warner Home Video, 2012.

Eyes on the Prize: America's Civil Rights Year.
PBS Home Video, 2010.

JFK: The Lost Bullet.
National Geographic, 2011.

The Kennedys.
A &E Television Networks, 2009.

The Kennedys.
Paramount Home Entertainment, 2008

PT 109.
Warner Brothers Entertainment, 2009.

Places to visit

Kennedy Memorial
Runnymede
Windsor Road, Old Windsor, Berkshire,
SL4 2JL
Phone: 01784 432891
www.nationaltrust.org.uk/runnymede/
things-to-see-and-do/page-1

Opened by Queen Elizabeth II in 1965, this memorial honors Kennedy. The queen gave one acre of ground around the memorial to the United States, technically making it U.S. land.

The Sixth Floor Museum at Dealey Plaza
411 Elm Street
Dallas, TX 75202
Phone: 214-747-6660
www.jfk.org

Housed in the building from which Lee Harvey Oswald shot JFK, the museum has many details about the assassination.

John Fitzgerald Kennedy
National Historic Site
83 Beals Street
Brookline, Massachusetts 02446
Phone: 617-566-7937
www.nps.gov/jofi/index.htm

This historic site is the home in which Kennedy was born in 1917. His mother Rose tried to make the house look as it did when the family lived there decades ago.

For further research

The space program
What were the three main parts of the U.S. space program during the 1960s? What were its successes and failures along the way? How was John F. Kennedy honored for his efforts to put humans on the moon?

Civil rights
What were some of the details of the two major civil rights laws passed in 1964 and 1965? What happened in many U.S. cities after the assassination of Martin Luther King Jr.?

The Cold War
What were some of the details of the 1963 treaty on testing nuclear weapons, signed by the Soviet Union, the United States, and the United Kingdom? What treaties followed in the 1970s and 1980s to further limit the building of nuclear weapons?

The assassination
Books and articles about the Kennedy killing appear often. What are some of the recent theories about who killed him and why?

Index